WITHDRAWN

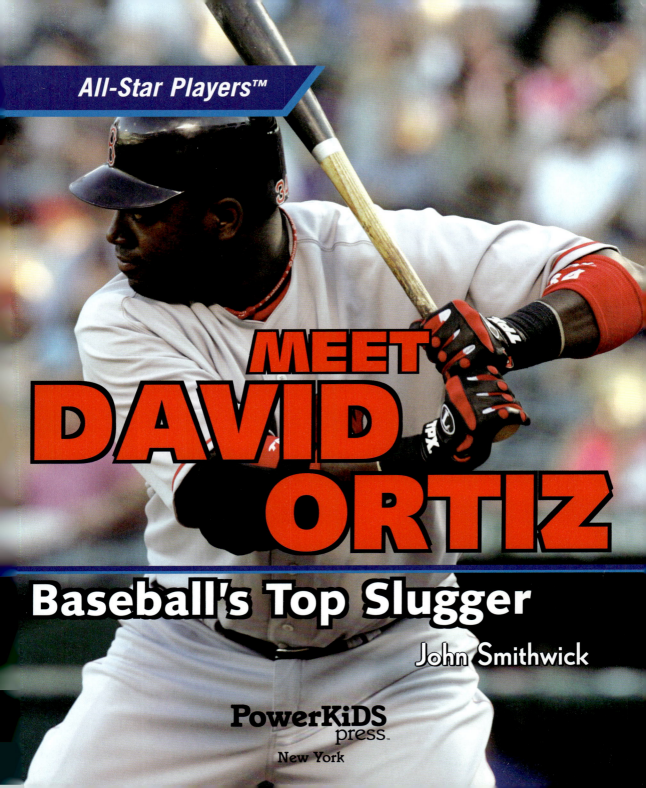

Published in 2007 by The Rosen Publishing Group, Inc.
29 East 21st Street, New York, NY 10010

Copyright © 2007 by The Rosen Publishing Group, Inc.

All rights reserved. No part of this book may be reproduced in any form without permission in writing from the publisher, except by a reviewer.

First Edition

Editor: Jennifer Way
Book Design: Greg Tucker
Photo Researcher: Sam Cha

Photo Credits: Cover, p. 1 © Ronald Martinez/Getty Images; p. 4 © Dave Sandford/Getty Images; p. 7 © John Raoux-Pool/Getty Images; p. 9 © Craig Melvin/Allsport; pp. 10, 13 © David Seelig/Stringer; p. 14 © Tom Pidgeon/Getty Images; p. 15 © Otto Greule Jr./Getty Images; pp. 16 (top), 26 (top), 29 © Jim McIsaac/Getty Images; p. 16 (bottom) © Doug Pensinger/Getty Images; p. 18 © Brian Bahr/Getty Images; pp. 19, 21 © Al Bello/Getty Images; p. 22 © Ezra Shaw/Getty Images; p. 23 © Stephan Dunn/Getty Images; p. 25 © Darren McCallester/Getty Images; p. 26 (bottom) © Eliot J. Schechter/Getty Images; p. 28 © Jonathan Daniel/Getty Images.

Library of Congress Cataloging-in-Publication Data

Smithwick, John.
   Meet David Ortiz : baseball's top slugger / John Smithwick. — 1st ed.
     p. cm. — (All-star players)
   Includes index.
   ISBN-13: 978-1-4042-3637-0 (library binding)
   ISBN-10: 1-4042-3637-6 (library binding)
   1. Ortiz, David, 1975– —Juvenile literature. 2. Baseball players—Dominican Republic—Biography—Juvenile literature.   I. Title.
   GV865.O78S65 2007
   796.357092—dc22
   [B]
                                                      2006021012

Manufactured in the United States of America

Contents

Meet Big Papi	5
Ortiz's Childhood	6
Playing in the Minor Leagues	8
The Minnesota Twins	12
The Boston Red Sox	17
The 2004 World Series	20
Big Papi off the Field	24
The Outlook for Ortiz	27
Stat Sheet	30
Glossary	31
Index	32
Web Sites	32

David Ortiz is a top designated hitter for the Boston Red Sox. Sometimes people who are great batters are called sluggers.

4

Meet Big Papi

David Ortiz is the **designated** hitter for the Boston Red Sox. A designated hitter is also called a DH. Most pitchers are not good hitters, so designated hitters are used to bat in their place. Designated hitters do not play in the field. Ortiz is one of the best and most **dramatic** designated hitters in Major League Baseball.

The Red Sox call Ortiz Big Papi. He got the first half of this nickname because of his size. He stands 6 feet 4 inches (1.9 m) tall. *Papi* is a **slang** term for "daddy" in Ortiz's native country, the Dominican Republic. The Red Sox call him Papi because he is one of the leaders of the team.

All-Star Stats

Ortiz has his own line of salsa, called Big Papi Salsa.

Ortiz's Childhood

Ortiz was born on November 18, 1975, in Santo Domingo, the capital of the Dominican Republic. David was the oldest of the four Ortiz children, and his parents trusted him to look after his younger siblings. This helped him build leadership skills at a young age.

David's father, Enrique, played **professional** baseball for a few teams in the Dominican Republic. David **inherited** his father's love and talent for the game. Since David was so tall and **athletic**, he also became a great basketball player at a young age.

Baseball remained his favorite sport, however. He was so good that he drew the attention of major-league scouts while he was still in high school. The Seattle Mariners **drafted** David in November 1992. He had just turned 17.

Ortiz is proud of his Dominican roots. Here he plays for the Dominican Republic at the World Baseball Classic in 2006.

Playing in the Minor Leagues

Even though the Mariners drafted him, they believed that Ortiz was too young and inexperienced to play on the major-league level. They sent him to the **minor leagues** to train as a first baseman. Each major-league team also has several minor-league teams. When a player improves, he advances through different minor-league levels. If he is good enough, he might one day be ready to play in the majors.

Ortiz struggled in his first minor-league season. He was used to playing baseball with other teenagers. Now he was facing pitchers who could throw 80 miles per hour (129 km/h). He struck out a lot.

Ortiz improved quickly. He collected 93 RBI in his third season. RBI stands for "runs batted in."

Ortiz struggled on the Mariners' minor-league team. The Minnesota Twins thought they could use a hitter like Ortiz and asked him to join their team in 1996.

Playing in the Minor Leagues

Playing in the Minor Leagues

These occur when there are players on base and the batter advances them home. A player with a high number of RBI is very valuable to his team.

As good as Ortiz was, he remained in the minors. The Mariners already had a designated hitter and a first baseman. However, scouts from the Minnesota Twins had been following Ortiz's career. The Twins had an aging DH, and they needed a good first baseman. In 1996, Ortiz moved to the Minnesota Twins.

Although Ortiz left the minor-league Mariners team to join the major-league Twins, his struggle to prove himself was not yet over.

The Minnesota Twins

Ortiz made his major-league **debut** with the Twins in September 1997. He hit a home run in his second game. Even though he had this excellent start, the Twins' management did not think Ortiz was ready to compete on the major-league level. He was sent back to the minor league.

In the spring of 2000, Ortiz was ready to leave his minor-league days behind him. He trained harder than he ever had before. This hard work paid off, and Ortiz joined the Twins again.

Over the next two seasons, Ortiz **injured** his left knee and broke his right wrist. The wrist injury affected his swing. As a result Ortiz's batting average was not what the Twins had in mind when they signed him. A batting average is the percentage of hits a player has per times at bat. A .300 average means a player got 3 hits in 10 attempts at the plate. Anything above .280 is

This picture of David Ortiz was taken while he played for the Minnesota Twins' minor-league team.

The Minnesota Twins

considered good. Ortiz's .272 average in the 2002 season was not bad, but the Twins wanted more from a designated hitter. The organization decided to let him go.

Ortiz might have returned to the minors if not for his friend Pedro Martinez. Martinez is also from the Dominican Republic and is one of the best pitchers in baseball.

Ortiz spent two seasons with the Twins' major-league team. Here he is in 2002.

The Minnesota Twins

He played for the Boston Red Sox. Martinez told the Red Sox general manager that the team should sign Ortiz. The general manager agreed, and Ortiz joined the Red Sox. Ortiz would soon make baseball history.

Ortiz's last season with the Twins was 2002. After that year his friend Pedro Martinez helped him become part of the Boston Red Sox.

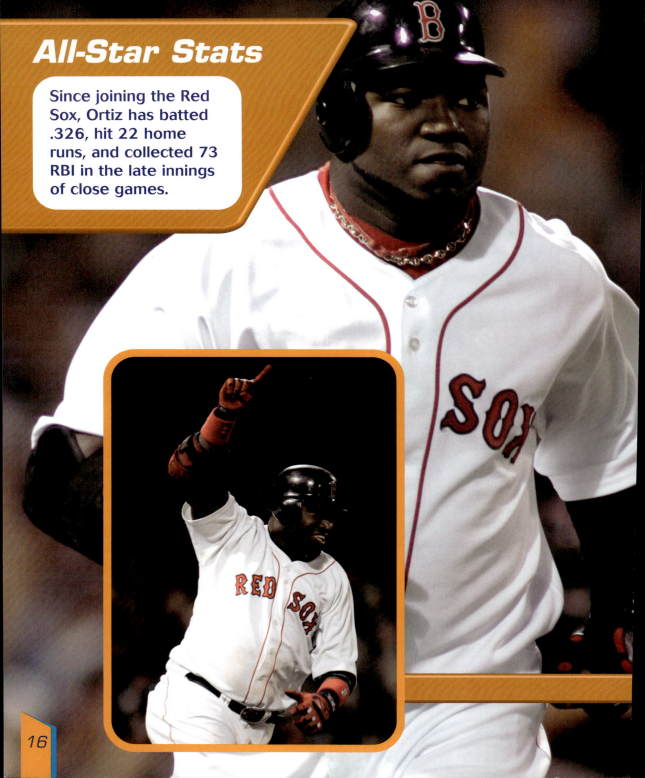

All-Star Stats

Since joining the Red Sox, Ortiz has batted .326, hit 22 home runs, and collected 73 RBI in the late innings of close games.

The Boston Red Sox

Ortiz had an immediate impact on his new team. The 2003 Red Sox were considered by many to be a team of **misfits** and **eccentrics**. Ortiz soon found himself in the position of team leader. He brought the team together in the locker room, and they began to play better together on the field. Ortiz led the Red Sox to the postseason in 2003.

The postseason has series, or groupings, of games in which the best teams from each region play one another. This leads to the World Series. The team that wins the World Series is that year's champion team.

In the 2003 postseason, the Red Sox won the American League Division Series against Oakland. Ortiz hit a two-run double in the final game of the series. The Red Sox then advanced to the next

Ortiz quickly became a valued member of the Red Sox. Inset: Ortiz is known for pointing to the sky when he scores a run.

The Boston Red Sox

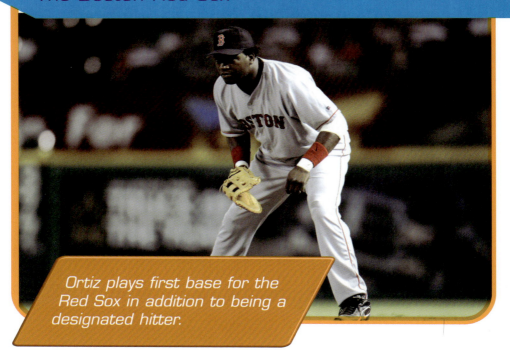

Ortiz plays first base for the Red Sox in addition to being a designated hitter.

round, the American League Championship Series. If they won this series, they would get to play in the World Series. The Red Sox faced their most bitter rival, the New York Yankees. The series was close, but in the end, the Red Sox lost to the Yankees.

There is a **superstition** in baseball called the Curse of the Bambino. The Bambino was Babe Ruth's nickname. The Red Sox had not won a

The Boston Red Sox

World Series since 1918, when they traded Ruth to the Yankees. Many fans, players, and coaches thought they would never win a World Series again. Ortiz and the Red Sox almost broke the curse in 2003. They wanted to break it for good the following year.

The Red Sox came close to breaking the Curse of the Bambino once they added Ortiz to their lineup.

The 2004 World Series

In 2004, Ortiz became known as a clutch hitter. A clutch hitter does well in tight situations. He can hit home runs late in the game or when his team is behind. Ortiz's batting often bailed the Red Sox out of trouble.

Ortiz hit .301 with 41 home runs in 2004. He collected 139 RBI, the second most in the American League. He also earned his first trip to the All-Star Game, in which he hit a two-run homer.

Once again Ortiz helped the Red Sox reach the postseason. Once again they faced the Yankees in the American League Championship Series.

When the Red Sox dropped the first three games, it looked like the Curse of the Bambino was real. They had to win the next four games or they would lose the series. No baseball team had ever come back from losing three games in

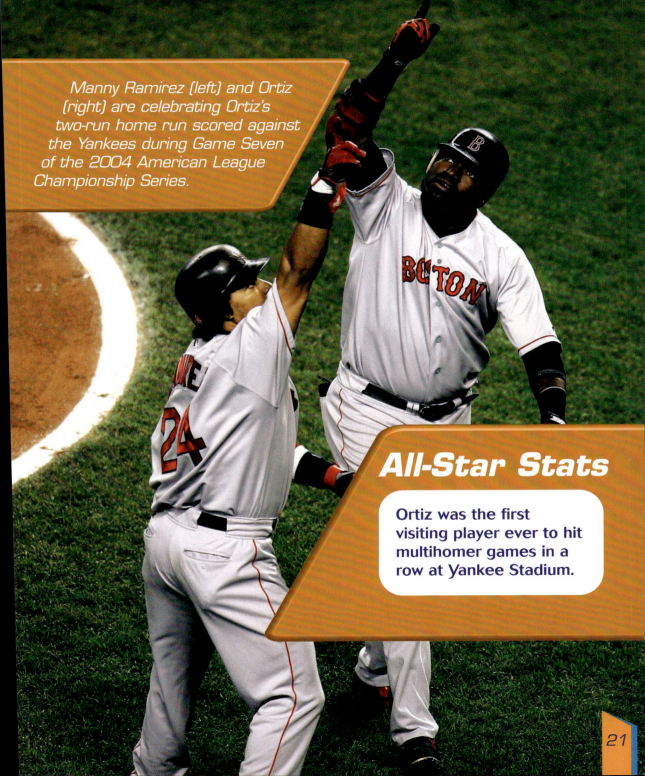

Manny Ramirez (left) and Ortiz (right) are celebrating Ortiz's two-run home run scored against the Yankees during Game Seven of the 2004 American League Championship Series.

All-Star Stats

Ortiz was the first visiting player ever to hit multihomer games in a row at Yankee Stadium.

The 2004 World Series

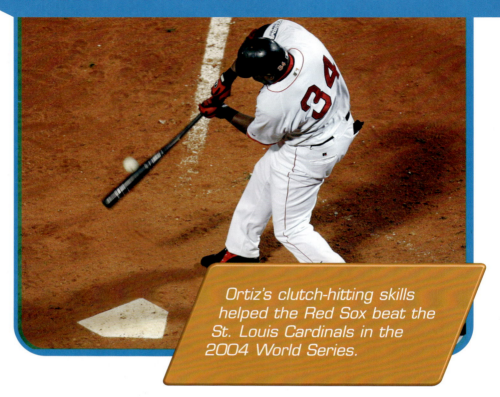

Ortiz's clutch-hitting skills helped the Red Sox beat the St. Louis Cardinals in the 2004 World Series.

the series. Ortiz won Game Four with a clutch home run in the twelfth inning. In Game Five he hit a game-winning single. In Game Seven he hit a home run in the first inning.

Thanks to Ortiz's efforts, the Red Sox finally beat the Yankees and proved that curses do not exist. They went on to **sweep** the St. Louis Cardinals in the 2004 World Series.

The 2004 World Series

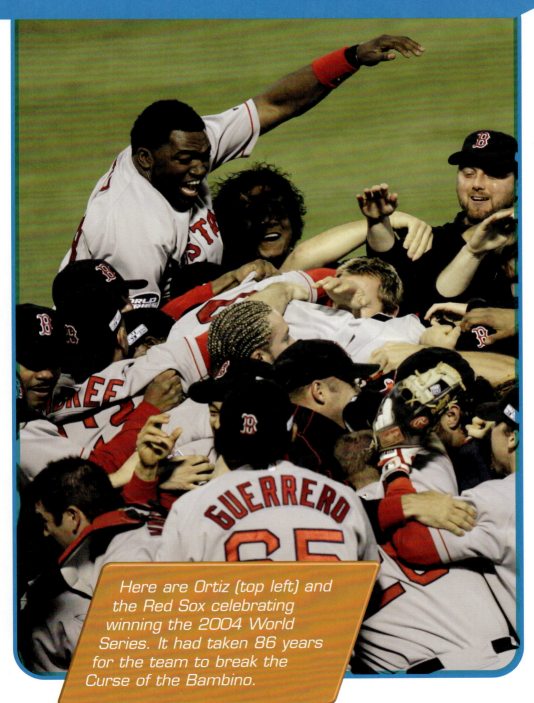

Here are Ortiz (top left) and the Red Sox celebrating winning the 2004 World Series. It had taken 86 years for the team to break the Curse of the Bambino.

Big Papi off the Field

Ortiz is a family man. He and his wife, Tiffany, have three children, named Yessica, Alexandra, and D'Angelo. D'Angelo is named for Ortiz's mother, Angela. She died in a car accident on New Year's Eve in 2002. Ortiz loved his mother very much. He says that he thinks about her every day. He always wears a gold chain around his neck that says RIP Angela.

In addition to hitting home runs, Ortiz is known for his smile and his easygoing nature. Lots of professional athletes feel **pressure** when the whole world is watching them. Ortiz has repeatedly claimed that he feels no pressure. He just relaxes and plays baseball. This quality makes him one of the most popular players on the team.

Big Papi off the Field

Ortiz is committed to helping others. He regularly gives baseball lessons to Boston-area children. He often appears at **celebrity** events to raise money for charities. Ortiz and the Red Sox work with the Jimmy Fund, a Boston-based **cancer** charity.

Here is Ortiz with his wife, Tiffany. She is from Wisconsin and has made her husband a fan of the Green Bay Packers football team.

Both the 2005 and 2006 seasons have been good ones for Ortiz.

26

The Outlook for Ortiz

Ortiz had his best season yet in 2005. He batted .300 and led the American League with 148 RBI. His 47 home runs were second in the American League to Alex Rodriguez's of the Yankees. Ortiz also finished second to Rodriguez in votes for the American League Most Valuable Player award. The Most Valuable Player, also known as the MVP, does more for his team than any other player in the league. The 2005 vote was **controversial**. Some of the voters thought Ortiz should be disqualified because he is a DH, which means that he does not get to contribute to his team's **defense**. It is rare for a DH to win as many MVP votes as Ortiz did. This shows what a popular and valued player he has become.

Ortiz (left) is a friend and a leader to his teammates. Here he is with Manny Ramirez.

The Outlook for Ortiz

Ortiz sometimes lends his batting talents to home run-hitting contests, such as this one held in 2005.

More importantly Ortiz remains a clutch hitter. In 2005, 20 of his 47 home runs either tied the game or put the Red Sox ahead. People who follow baseball believe that Ortiz's leadership skills, easygoing nature, and numerous home runs will continue to bring together his teammates for many seasons to come.

Ortiz hopes to help the Red Sox win games for years to come.

Stat Sheet

Height: 6'4" (1.9 m)
Weight: 230 pounds (104 kg)
Team: Boston Red Sox
Uniform Number: 34
Date of Birth: November 18, 1975
Years in MLB: 9

2005 Season Stats

Batting Average	Home Runs	RBI
.300	47	148

Glossary

athletic (ath-LEH-tik) Having ability and training in sports and exercises of strength.

cancer (KAN-ser) A sickness in which cells multiply out of control and do not work properly.

celebrity (seh-LEH-breh-tee) A famous person.

controversial (kon-truh-VUR-shul) Causing disagreement.

debut (DAY-byoo) A first public appearance, as of a performer.

defense (DEE-fents) When a team tries to stop the other team from scoring.

designated (DEH-zig-nayt-ed) Chosen for a special task.

drafted (DRAFT-ed) Selected someone for a special purpose.

dramatic (druh-MAT-ik) Striking in appearance and effect.

eccentrics (ik-SEN-triks) People who are strange or different from most other people.

inherited (in-HER-it-ed) Received something from a parent.

injured (IN-jurd) Harmed or hurt a person's body.

minor leagues (MY-nur LEEGZ) Groups of teams on which players play before they are good enough for the next level.

misfits (MIS-fits) People who are different from others.

pressure (PREH-shur) The weight of feeling worried about something.

professional (pruh-FESH-nul) Paid to do something.

slang (SLANG) Words that are used in informal speech.

superstition (soo-pur-STIH-shun) A belief that something is unlucky.

sweep (SWEEP) To win all stages of a game or contest.

Index

B
Boston Red Sox, 5, 15, 17–20, 22, 25, 28

D
defense, 27
designated hitter(s) (DH), 5, 11, 14, 27
Dominican Republic, 5–6, 14

F
first baseman, 8, 11

J
Jimmy Fund, 25

M
Major League Baseball, 5
Minnesota Twins, 11–12, 14
minor league(s), 8, 12
misfits, 17

N
New York Yankees, 18–20, 22, 27

O
Ortiz, Angela (mother), 24
Ortiz, Enrique (father), 6
Ortiz, Tiffany (wife), 24

S
Seattle Mariners, 6, 8, 11
St. Louis Cardinals, 22
superstition, 18

Web Sites

Due to the changing nature of Internet links, PowerKids Press has developed an online list of Web sites related to the subject of this book. This site is updated regularly. Please use this link to access the list:
www.powerkidslinks.com/asp/david/

WITHDRAWN